Better Homes and Gardens®

QUICK MAIN DISHES

Our seal assures you that every recipe in *Quick Main Dishes*
has been tested in the Better Homes and Gardens® Test Kitchen.
This means that each recipe is practical and reliable,
and meets our high standards of taste appeal.

For years, Better Homes and Gardens® Books has been a leader in publishing cook books. In *Quick Main Dishes,* we've pulled together a delicious collection of recipes from several of our latest best-sellers. These no-fail recipes will make your cooking easier and more enjoyable.

Editor: Rosemary C. Hutchinson
Editorial Project Manager: James D. Blume
Graphic Designer: Harijs Priekulis
Electronic Text Processor: Paula Forest

On the front cover: Skillet Taco Pizza *(see recipe, page 14)*

First Edition. First Printing.
ISBN: 0-696-01860-8

Contents

Orange-Curried Lamb

Total Time: 20 minutes

¾	**pound boneless lamb**
½	**cup chicken broth**
½	**cup orange juice**
1	**tablespoon cornstarch**
1	**tablespoon curry powder**
⅛	**teaspoon salt**
⅛	**teaspoon onion powder**

● Cut the lamb on the bias into thin bite-size strips. For sauce, stir together chicken broth, orange juice, cornstarch, curry powder, salt, and onion powder. Set aside.

In a hurry? Try our curry. Stir-fried lamb strips, pea pods, and tomatoes cook in a flash.

1	**tablespoon cooking oil**

● Preheat a wok or 12-inch skillet over high heat. Add the cooking oil. (Add more oil as necessary during cooking.) Add lamb to wok or skillet. Stir-fry about 3 minutes or till lamb is no longer pink. Push from center of wok.

1	**6-ounce package frozen pea pods**
1	**medium tomato, cut into thin wedges**
½	**cup peanuts**
½	**cup raisins**
	Hot cooked couscous *or* **rice**

● Stir sauce. Add sauce to the center of the wok or skillet. Cook and stir till thickened and bubbly. Stir meat into sauce. Stir in pea pods, tomato, peanuts, and raisins. Cook about 2 minutes more or till heated through. Serve over couscous or rice. Makes 4 servings.

Easy Ground Beef Stir-Fry

Total Time: 15 minutes

½ cup cold water
3 tablespoons soy sauce
1 tablespoon cornstarch
½ teaspoon ground ginger
⅛ teaspoon garlic powder

● For sauce, stir together cold water, soy sauce, cornstarch, ginger, and garlic powder. Set aside.

1 10-ounce package frozen cut broccoli
1 tablespoon cooking oil

● Run water over broccoli to thaw. Pat dry with paper towels. Preheat a wok or large skillet over high heat. Add cooking oil. (Add more oil as necessary during cooking.) Stir-fry broccoli for 2 to 3 minutes or till crisp-tender. Remove broccoli from the wok.

1 pound lean ground beef
1 8-ounce can sliced water chestnuts, drained

● Crumble *half* of the ground beef into the hot wok or skillet. Stir-fry about 2 minutes or till beef loses its pink color. Remove beef. Stir-fry remaining beef about 2 minutes. Drain off fat. Return all beef and broccoli to the wok. Stir in water chestnuts. Push from the center of the wok or skillet.

Hot cooked rice

● Stir the sauce. Add sauce to the center of the wok. Cook and stir till thickened and bubbly. Cook and stir for 2 minutes more. Serve with hot cooked rice. Makes 4 servings.

Put your knife away. Ground beef, frozen cut broccoli, and canned sliced water chestnuts make this a chop-free stir-fry dish.

Lemon-Sauced Pork

Total Time: 20 minutes

¾ **pound boneless pork**
½ **cup cold water**
¼ **cup dry white wine**
2 **tablespoons soy sauce**
1 **tablespoon cornstarch**
1 **teaspoon instant chicken bouillon granules**
½ **teaspoon finely shredded lemon peel**

● Cut pork on the bias into thin bite-size strips. For sauce, stir together water, wine, soy sauce, cornstarch, bouillon granules, and lemon peel. Set aside.

A little lemon peel provides the fresh lemon flavor in this stir-fry dish.

1 **10-ounce package frozen cut asparagus**
1 **tablespoon cooking oil**
1 **small onion, thinly sliced**
1 **8-ounce can sliced water chestnuts, drained**

● Run water over frozen asparagus to thaw (see photo, below). Pat dry with paper towels. Preheat a wok or large skillet over high heat. Add cooking oil. (Add more oil as necessary during cooking.) Add asparagus and onion. Stir-fry about 3 minutes or till crisp-tender. Remove vegetables.
   Add pork to hot wok. Stir-fry about 3 minutes or till no longer pink. Return vegetables to wok. Stir in water chestnuts. Push from center of the wok.

Hot cooked rice

● Stir sauce. Add to center of wok. Cook and stir till thickened and bubbly. Cook and stir for 2 minutes more. Serve over rice. Makes 4 servings.

To quick-thaw frozen vegetables, place the frozen vegetables in a colander. Run hot tap water over the vegetables till thawed. Drain well. For stir-frying, pat the vegetables dry with paper towels to prevent spattering.

Butterfly Pork Chops with Apple Rings

Total Time: 25 minutes

4	pork loin butterfly chops, cut ½ inch thick
2	tablespoons margarine *or* butter

● Trim excess fat from chops. Season chops with pepper. In a large skillet melt margarine or butter. Add chops to skillet. Cook over medium heat about 5 minutes or till brown, turning once.

You won't have a bone to pick with these chops. Boneless butterfly pork chops are perfect for panfrying because they're so tender.

1	6-ounce can (⅔ cup) apple juice
2	tablespoons raisins
½	teaspoon instant chicken bouillon granules
	Dash ground cinnamon
	Dash ground cloves
2	medium apples, cored and cut into rings

● Add apple juice, raisins, bouillon granules, cinnamon, and cloves. Bring to boiling. Reduce heat. Cover and simmer 5 minutes. Add apple rings. Simmer about 5 minutes more or till pork is no longer pink. Transfer chops and apples to a serving platter. Keep warm.

1	tablespoon cold water
2	teaspoons cornstarch

● Combine water and cornstarch. Stir into juices in the skillet. Cook and stir till thickened and bubbly. Cook and stir for 2 minutes more. Spoon sauce over chops and apple rings. Makes 4 servings.

Beefy Tomato-Rice Dinner

Total Time: 30 minutes

1 pound ground beef	● In a large saucepan cook ground beef till brown. Drain off fat.
1 16-ounce can tomatoes, cut up 1 9-ounce package frozen cut green beans 1 8-ounce can tomato sauce 1 cup water 1 6-ounce package regular curry-flavored rice mix with raisins and almonds	● Stir in *undrained* tomatoes, green beans, tomato sauce, water, and rice and seasoning packet. Bring to boiling. Reduce heat. Cover and simmer about 25 minutes or till beans are crisp-tender and rice is tender. Sprinkle with almonds from rice mix. Makes 4 servings.

Once you assemble this one-dish meal, let it simmer away while you put your feet up and relax.

Sauerbraten Pork Steaks

Total Time: 20 minutes

1 tablespoon cooking oil 4 pork *or* beef cubed steaks	● Heat a large skillet over high heat. Add cooking oil to skillet. Cook steaks in hot oil about 8 minutes or till meat is no longer pink, turning once. Remove steaks and keep warm. Drain fat from skillet.
¾ cup chicken broth ¼ cup finely chopped celery 1 tablespoon brown sugar 1 tablespoon vinegar 1 teaspoon prepared mustard ¼ teaspoon salt Dash pepper 2 tablespoons crushed gingersnaps (2 cookies) Hot cooked noodles	● In the same skillet stir together chicken broth, celery, brown sugar, vinegar, mustard, salt, and pepper. Stir in gingersnaps. Cook and stir till mixture is thick and bubbly. Serve meat and sauce over hot cooked noodles. Serves 4.

We borrowed the flavor of traditional German pot roast for these cubed steaks.

Pork Medaillons with
Apricots

Pork Medaillons With Apricots

Total Time: 20 minutes

1 pound pork tenderloin 1 tablespoon margarine *or* butter	● Cut pork tenderloin crosswise into 1-inch-thick slices. Season with salt and pepper. In a 12-inch skillet cook pork in margarine or butter over medium heat about 5 minutes or till brown on both sides, turning once.
1 12-ounce can apricot nectar ¼ cup quartered dried apricots 3 green onions, sliced 1 teaspoon instant chicken bouillon granules ¼ teaspoon ground ginger 2 tablespoons water 1 tablespoon cornstarch Hot cooked noodles	● Add apricot nectar, apricots, green onions, chicken bouillon granules, and ginger. Bring mixture to boiling. Reduce heat. Cover and simmer about 5 minutes or till pork is no longer pink. Remove pork from skillet and keep warm. Meanwhile, combine water and cornstarch. Add cornstarch mixture to skillet. Cook and stir till thickened and bubbly. Cook and stir for 2 minutes more. Serve pork and apricot sauce over noodles. Makes 4 servings.

You *can* have it all. This tangy-sauced pork is quick to make, delicious, and elegant.

Beef with Marsala

Total Time: 25 minutes

2 beef top loin steaks, cut 1 inch thick (about 1½ pounds total) 3 tablespoons margarine *or* butter 1 large onion, sliced and separated into rings (1 cup)	● Cut steaks in half crosswise. In a 12-inch skillet melt the margarine or butter. Add the onion and cook over medium heat till tender but not brown. Remove with a slotted spoon. Add steaks to skillet and cook for 5 minutes. Turn steaks. Cook to desired doneness (allow 5 to 7 minutes for medium doneness). Remove steaks from skillet. Keep warm.
½ cup dry marsala ⅓ cup water 2 tablespoons snipped parsley ¼ teaspoon salt ⅛ teaspoon pepper	● For sauce, add the cooked onion, wine, water, parsley, salt, and pepper to drippings in skillet. Bring to boiling. Cook, uncovered, for 2 to 3 minutes or till slightly reduced, stirring to scrape brown bits from bottom of skillet. Remove from heat.
4 slices French bread, cut ¾ inch thick and toasted	● To serve, place a toasted bread slice on each of 4 dinner plates. Top each with a piece of steak. Spoon some of the sauce over each serving. Pass remaining sauce. Makes 4 servings.

When you want to put your best food forward, bring out this exceptional dish—steak and onions served over toasted French bread and topped with a marsala sauce.

Sausage and Cabbage

Total Time: 18 minutes

1 **pound fully cooked Polish sausage *or* other smoked sausage** ¼ **cup water** 1 **teaspoon instant chicken bouillon granules**	● In a 12-inch skillet combine sausage, water, and bouillon granules. Cover and cook over medium heat for 5 minutes.
1 **small head cabbage** 2 **cups frozen crinkle-cut carrots**	● Meanwhile, cut cabbage into 4 wedges. Remove core. Coarsely shred wedges. Add cabbage and carrots to the skillet. Cover and cook about 10 minutes or till the vegetables are crisp-tender.
½ **cup dairy sour cream** ½ **teaspoon caraway seed**	● Stir sour cream and caraway seed into cabbage mixture. Cover and cook about 3 minutes or till heated through. *Do not boil.* Makes 4 servings.

One large sausage link or several smaller individual links work equally well in this dish. If you have a large link, cut it into 3- to 4-inch lengths.

Franks and Taters

Total Time: 20 minutes

½ **of a 24-ounce package (3 cups) frozen hash brown potatoes with onion and peppers** 1 **9-ounce package frozen French-style green beans** ½ **cup water**	● In a large skillet combine potatoes, green beans, and water. Cover and cook about 5 minutes or till vegetables are just tender. Drain.
1 **16-ounce package frankfurters *or* one 12-ounce package fully cooked smoked sausage links** ½ **cup milk** 1 **teaspoon cornstarch** 1 **cup shredded cheddar cheese (4 ounces)**	● Meanwhile, cut frankfurters or sausage links into 1-inch pieces. Add meat to potato mixture. Combine milk and cornstarch. Stir into skillet. Cook and stir till boiling. Stir in *half* of the cheese. Reduce heat to low. Cover and simmer about 5 minutes or till heated through. Sprinkle with the remaining cheese. Serves 4 to 6.

Cooking with fresh vegetables can mean extra minutes in the kitchen. So take advantage of the convenience of frozen potatoes and green beans and try this skillet dinner.

Sausage-Macaroni Skillet

Total Time: 30 minutes

1 8-ounce package brown-and-serve sausage links	● In a large skillet cook sausage for 6 to 8 minutes or till brown, turning to cook evenly on all sides. Remove sausage. Drain fat from skillet.
1 16-ounce can tomatoes, cut up 1 7¼-ounce package macaroni-and-cheese dinner mix 1 cup water ¼ cup chopped onion	● In the same skillet combine *undrained* tomatoes, macaroni from the dinner mix, water, and onion. Bring to boiling; reduce heat. Cover and simmer for 10 to 12 minutes or till macaroni is tender, stirring occasionally.
¼ cup margarine *or* butter ¼ cup milk	● Meanwhile, cut sausage links into thirds. Stir cheese sauce packet from mix, margarine or butter, and milk into macaroni mixture. Stir in sausage and cook about 5 minutes more or till heated through. Makes 4 servings.

Recipes like this one can be a lifesaver on days when you're on the run and too busy to plan dinner. Just keep the ingredients on hand and you can serve this tasty one-dish meal in a half hour.

Polish Sausage With Beans

Total Time: 15 minutes

8 ounces fully cooked Polish sausage *or* one 8-ounce package frankfurters	● Cut the Polish sausage or frankfurters into 1-inch pieces.
1 8½-ounce can lima beans, drained 1 8-ounce can pork and beans with tomato sauce 1 8-ounce can red kidney beans, drained ¼ cup catsup 1 tablespoon brown sugar 1 tablespoon vinegar ⅛ teaspoon onion powder Dash dry mustard Dash bottled hot pepper sauce	● In a medium saucepan combine lima beans, pork and beans, kidney beans, catsup, brown sugar, vinegar, onion powder, dry mustard, and hot pepper sauce. Stir in the sausage. Bring to boiling. Reduce heat. Simmer about 5 minutes or till heated through. Serves 3.

When you're in a tighter-than-usual time crunch, substitute ⅓ cup bottled barbecue sauce for the catsup, brown sugar, and vinegar.

Total Time: 30 minutes

Skillet Taco Pizza

¾ pound ground beef
1 8-ounce can pizza sauce
1 teaspoon chili powder
⅛ teaspoon ground red
    pepper
1 package (10) refrigerated
    biscuits

● In a skillet cook beef till browned. Drain. Stir in pizza sauce, chili powder, and pepper. Heat through. Keep warm.

Meanwhile, lightly grease a heavy 10-inch skillet. Press biscuits into the bottom and up the sides of the skillet (see photo, below top). Moisten edges of biscuits with water and pinch to seal. Cook, covered, over medium-low heat for 2 minutes. Check crust and seal any holes by pressing biscuits together with a fork.

Pictured on the cover.

Pizza in minutes—without heating up the kitchen.

1 cup shredded mozzarella
    cheese (4 ounces)
1 cup shredded lettuce
1 medium tomato, chopped
½ cup sliced pitted ripe
    olives (optional)
½ cup coarsely crushed
    tortilla chips

● Spoon beef mixture atop crust in the skillet. Cook, covered, 9 minutes. Sprinkle with cheese. Cook, covered, over medium-low heat for 2 to 3 minutes or till cheese is melted. Remove from heat. Top with lettuce; tomato; olives, if desired; and tortilla chips (see photo, below bottom). Makes 4 servings.

To make the biscuit crust, with greased hands, press biscuits into the bottom and about ½ inch up the sides of the skillet. Moisten edges with water and pinch together tightly.

Just before serving, top the pizza with shredded lettuce; tomato; olives, if desired; and crushed tortilla chips. Then serve it at the table, right from the skillet.

Walnut-Orange Chicken

Total Time: 25 minutes

⅔ cup long grain rice
2 whole large skinned and
　　boned chicken breasts
½ cup orange juice
2 tablespoons soy sauce
1 tablespoon dry sherry
1½ teaspoons cornstarch
1 teaspoon grated fresh
　　gingerroot
½ cup chopped walnuts

● Cook rice according to package directions. Meanwhile, cut the chicken into 1-inch pieces. For sauce, in a small mixing bowl stir together the orange juice, soy sauce, dry sherry, cornstarch, and gingerroot. Set mixture aside.

In a 10-inch skillet cook walnuts over medium heat till toasted, stirring frequently. Remove nuts.

Fresh orange segments, toasted walnuts, and a hint of gingerroot blended with chicken are a flavor sensation certain to be a hit at your house.

2 tablespoons cooking oil
2 green onions, thinly sliced
1 orange, peeled, separated
　　into segments, and cut
　　into pieces

● Add cooking oil to the hot skillet. Stir-fry onions for 30 seconds. Add *half* of the chicken. Stir-fry for 2 to 3 minutes or till chicken is no longer pink. Remove chicken and onions. Stir-fry remaining chicken for 2 to 3 minutes or till done. Return chicken and onions to skillet.

Stir sauce and add to skillet. Cook and stir till mixture is thickened and bubbly. Cook for 1 to 2 minutes more. Stir in walnuts and orange segments. Serve over rice. Makes 4 servings.

Jarlsberg Turkey

Total Time: 20 minutes

¼ cup all-purpose flour
½ teaspoon lemon pepper *or*
　　pepper
⅓ cup fine dry bread crumbs
⅓ cup finely shredded
　　Jarlsberg *or* Swiss
　　cheese (1½ ounces)
4 turkey breast slices
　　(about 8 ounces)
1 beaten egg

● In a plastic bag combine the flour and lemon pepper or pepper. In a shallow dish stir together the bread crumbs and shredded cheese.

One at a time, add turkey slices to flour mixture and shake to coat. Dip turkey slices into the egg and then into the cheese mixture, coating evenly.

Wonderful for cooking, Jarlsberg cheese is a Swiss-like cheese from Norway, with a nutty, slightly buttery flavor. It's the headliner in this crispy coating for turkey breast slices.

3 tablespoons margarine
　　or butter
1 lemon, cut into wedges

● In a large skillet melt margarine or butter. Cook turkey slices over medium heat about 4 minutes or till turkey is lightly browned on both sides and no longer pink, turning once. Serve with lemon wedges. Makes 4 servings.

Creamy Chicken And Broccoli

Total Time: 25 minutes

4 **eggs**	● Place eggs in a small saucepan. Add *warm* water to cover. Bring to boiling over high heat. Reduce the heat. Simmer, covered, for 15 minutes. Pour off hot water. Fill saucepan with *cold* water. Let stand for 2 minutes. Peel and slice eggs.
1 **10-ounce package frozen broccoli *or* asparagus spears**	
	Meanwhile, cook broccoli or asparagus spears according to package directions. Drain well. Keep warm.

2 **tablespoons margarine *or* butter**	● In a medium saucepan melt margarine over medium heat. Add almonds. Cook, stirring occasionally, till nuts are toasted. Stir in the flour, bouillon granules, salt, and pepper. Add milk all at once. Cook and stir over medium heat till thickened and bubbly. Cook and stir for 1 minute more. Stir in the chicken. Heat through.
¼ **cup slivered almonds**	
2 **tablespoons all-purpose flour**	
1 **teaspoon instant chicken bouillon granules**	
¼ **teaspoon salt**	
⅛ **teaspoon pepper**	
1 **cup milk**	
1½ **cups cubed cooked chicken**	
8 **rusks**	For each serving, place *one-fourth* of the broccoli over *two* rusks. Spoon *one-fourth* of the chicken mixture atop. Top with some of the egg slices and parsley. Makes 4 servings.
Snipped parsley	

If you find the sauce for this upscale creamed chicken on rusks a bit thick, thin it slightly by adding one or two tablespoons more milk.

Sweet 'n' Sour Skillet Burgers

Total Time: 35 minutes

4 **ounces wide noodles (3 cups)**	● Cook noodles according to package directions. Drain.

1 **beaten egg**	● Meanwhile, in a large bowl combine egg, bread crumbs, raisins, onion, and ¼ teaspoon *salt*. Add ground turkey. Mix well. Shape meat mixture into four ¾-inch-thick patties. In a 10-inch skillet cook patties in hot oil over medium heat for 5 minutes, turning once. Drain.
¼ **cup fine dry bread crumbs**	
¼ **cup raisins**	
2 **teaspoons dried minced onion**	
1 **pound ground raw turkey**	
1 **tablespoon cooking oil**	

1 **8-ounce can tomato sauce**	● For sauce, mix tomato sauce, apple cider or juice, brown sugar, mustard, and cloves. Pour over burgers in skillet. Cook, covered, over medium-low heat for 8 to 10 minutes or till meat is no longer pink. Remove burgers. Keep warm.
⅔ **cup apple cider *or* juice**	
1 **teaspoon brown sugar**	
¼ **teaspoon dry mustard**	
Dash ground cloves	

2 **gingersnaps, finely crushed (2 tablespoons)**	● Stir gingersnaps into sauce. Cook and stir 1 to 2 minutes or till bubbly. Serve burgers over noodles with some of the sauce. Pass remaining sauce. Serves 4.

Styled after German sauerbraten, these burgers have a delightfully different sweet and sour flavor. The crushed gingersnaps add a hint of sweetness and help thicken the sauce as well.

**Creamy Chicken
and Broccoli**

20-Minute Paella

20-Minute Paella

Total Time: 20 minutes

1 cup diced cooked chicken
½ cup long grain rice
¼ cup frozen peas
¼ cup frozen chopped onion
1 teaspoon instant chicken bouillon granules
¼ teaspoon bottle minced garlic *or* dash of garlic powder
⅛ teaspoon ground saffron *or* ground turmeric
Dash ground red pepper

● In a medium saucepan combine 1 cup *hot water,* chicken, rice, frozen peas, frozen onion, bouillon granules, garlic, saffron or turmeric, and red pepper. Bring to boiling, then reduce heat. Cover and cook over low heat for 13 minutes.

Frozen, shelled cooked shrimp work well, too. Just remember—place them in the refrigerator the night before to thaw.

6 ounces shrimp cooked in shells
½ of a 7¾-ounce can artichoke hearts
1 tablespoon diced pimiento

● While rice mixture is cooking, remove shells from shrimp. If artichoke hearts are marinated, drain and rinse them. Then stir the shrimp, artichokes, and pimiento into the cooked rice mixture. Cover and cook for 1 to 2 minutes more or till shrimp are heated through. Makes 2 servings.

Seafood Primavera

Total Time: 18 minutes

1 5-ounce package corkscrew macaroni with vegetables and cream sauce *or* one 4½-ounce package noodles with Parmesan cheese sauce
1½ cups loose-pack frozen mixed zucchini, carrots, cauliflower, lima beans, and Italian beans, *or* frozen mixed cauliflower, broccoli, and carrots
½ teaspoon dried basil, crushed

● Cook pasta mix according to package directions, *except* add frozen mixed vegetables and basil to the boiling water with the pasta mix.

Next time, instead of crab-flavored fish sticks, try using one 8-ounce package frozen peeled and deveined shrimp. Just add them to the boiling pasta mixture during the last 2 minutes of cooking.

8 ounces crab-flavored fish sticks
1 3-ounce package cream cheese
1 medium tomato

● While pasta mix is cooking, cut crab-flavored fish sticks into 1-inch pieces. Cut cream cheese into cubes. Cut tomato into wedges. Add fish-stick pieces to pasta mixture. Then add cream cheese to the pasta mixture. Cook, covered, over low heat about 2 minutes more or till cream cheese is melted and fish is heated through. To serve, spoon onto plates and garnish with tomato wedges. Makes 3 servings.

Veggie-Stuffed Steak

Total Time: 25 minutes

2	tablespoons margarine *or* butter
1	small potato, peeled and shredded
1	small carrot, shredded
1	green onion, chopped
¼	cup grated Parmesan cheese

● In a medium saucepan melt the margarine or butter. Add potato, carrot, and onion. Cook till tender, stirring occasionally. Remove from heat. Stir in Parmesan cheese. Cool slightly.

A vegetable trio, accompanied by grated Parmesan cheese, performs flavorfully in this broiled steak.

1	1½- to 2-pound beef top loin steak, cut 1 to 1½ inches thick

● Meanwhile, cut the steak in half crosswise. Cut a large slit horizontally in each half to form a pocket. Spoon the vegetable mixture into the pockets. Secure openings with wooden skewers or toothpicks. Season with salt and pepper.

● Place steaks on the unheated rack of a broiler pan. Broil 4 to 5 inches from the heat for 6 minutes. Turn steaks and broil to desired doneness (allow 6 to 8 minutes for medium). Remove skewers or toothpicks. Cut into serving-size pieces. Makes 4 servings.

Lamb Chops With Plum Sauce

Total Time: 20 minutes

½ cup plum jelly
2 green onions, sliced
2 tablespoons dry sherry
2 tablespoons soy sauce
1 tablespoon cornstarch
1 tablespoon lemon juice

8 lamb rib *or* loin chops *or*
  4 leg sirloin chops, cut
  ¾ inch thick

● For sauce, in a small saucepan combine jelly, green onions, sherry, soy sauce, cornstarch, and lemon juice. Cook and stir till thickened and bubbly. Cook and stir for 1 to 2 minutes more. Remove from heat.

● Slash the fat edges of chops in several places. Place chops on the unheated rack of a broiler pan. Brush with some of the sauce. Broil chops 3 to 4 inches from the heat for 5 minutes. Turn chops. Brush with additional sauce. Broil to desired doneness (allow 5 to 7 minutes for medium). Pass remaining sauce. Makes 4 servings.

Take a tip from our Test Kitchen: Turn chops with tongs instead of a fork. A fork will pierce the meat, allowing the juices to escape and causing the meat to dry out.

Orange-Molasses Pork Chops

Total Time: 15 minutes

3 pork loin chops, cut ½ inch thick Salt Pepper	● Place chops on the unheated rack of a broiler pan. Sprinkle with salt and pepper. Broil chops 3 to 4 inches from the heat for 6 minutes. Turn chops. Season with salt and pepper. Broil 6 to 7 minutes more or till no longer pink.
1 green onion, thinly sliced 1 tablespoon water ¼ teaspoon finely shredded orange peel 1 tablespoon orange juice 1 tablespoon catsup 1 tablespoon molasses Orange slices (optional)	● For sauce, during the last few minutes of broiling, in a small saucepan stir together onion, water, orange peel, orange juice, catsup, and molasses. Stir sauce over medium heat for 1 to 2 minutes or till hot. Serve sauce with chops. Garnish with orange slices, if desired. Makes 3 servings.

Satisfy a craving for barbecued chops by taking a few minutes to start a fire. Grill chops over *medium* coals on an uncovered grill for 5 minutes. Turn and grill for 6 to 7 minutes more or till no longer pink.

Pork and Turkey Burgers

Total Time: 25 minutes

3 green onions, thinly sliced 1 tablespoon frozen orange juice concentrate 2 teaspoons Worcestershire sauce ¼ teaspoon salt Dash pepper ½ pound ground turkey ½ pound ground pork	● In a medium mixing bowl combine onions, orange juice concentrate, Worcestershire sauce, salt, and pepper. Add turkey and pork. Mix well. Shape into four ½-inch-thick patties.
2 tablespoons bottled sweet-and-sour barbecue sauce *or* regular barbecue sauce 4 hamburger buns, split (optional)	● Place patties on the unheated rack of a broiler pan. Broil 3 to 4 inches from the heat for 10 to 12 minutes or till no longer pink, turning once and drizzling sauce over patties during the last few minutes of cooking. If desired, serve on buns. Makes 4 servings.

Broiling is a great way to lighten up your meals. When you cook food on a rack using direct heat, much of the fat drains away, but the juices and flavor stay inside.

Lime-Pepper Chicken

Total Time: 45 minutes

½ teaspoon finely shredded lime peel
⅓ cup lime juice
2 tablespoons cooking oil
1 teaspoon dried thyme, crushed
1 teaspoon cracked black pepper
½ teaspoon garlic salt

● For sauce, in a small mixing bowl stir together lime peel, lime juice, cooking oil, thyme, pepper, and garlic salt. Set mixture aside.

2 to 2½ pounds meaty chicken pieces (breasts, wings, thighs, and drumsticks)

● Place chicken, skin side down, on the unheated rack of a broiler pan. Brush with sauce. Broil 4 to 5 inches from the heat for 15 to 18 minutes or till lightly browned, brushing often with sauce. Turn chicken. Brush with sauce. Broil for 10 to 15 minutes more or till no longer pink, brushing often with sauce. Serves 4.

To grill, prepare the recipe as directed, *except* grill the chicken pieces, skin side down, on an uncovered grill, directly over *medium* coals for 20 minutes, brushing occasionally with sauce. Turn and grill for 10 to 20 minutes more or till done, brushing often with sauce.

Broiled Chicken Cordon Bleu

Total Time: 14 minutes

2 boned skinless chicken breast halves *or* turkey breast tenderloins (about 8 ounces total)
1 tablespoon soft *or* whipped margarine
2 slices process Swiss cheese (2 ounces)

● Place poultry on the unheated rack of a broiler pan. Brush with *half* of the margarine. Broil 4 inches from the heat for 4 minutes. Turn poultry over and brush with remaining margarine. Broil for 4 to 5 minutes more or till tender. Meanwhile, cut cheese slices in half.

So elegant, it's hard to believe this dish takes less than 15 minutes to make.

Coarse-grain brown mustard *or* Dijon-style mustard
2 thin slices fully cooked ham *or* Canadian-style bacon

● Brush tops of poultry with mustard. Place one-half slice of cheese on top of each piece of poultry, then top with the ham or bacon. (If necessary, cut ham slice to fit poultry.) Broil about 30 seconds or till ham is warm. Then top with remaining cheese. Broil for ½ to 1 minute more or till cheese is melted.

Paprika
Cherry tomatoes (optional)
Parsley sprigs (optional)

● To serve, transfer to dinner plates. Sprinkle with paprika. If desired, garnish with tomatoes and parsley. Makes 2 servings.

Mediterranean Turkey Burgers

Total Time: 25 minutes

1 beaten egg
½ cup soft bread crumbs
¼ cup chopped, pitted ripe olives
1 tablespoon dried parsley flakes
¼ teaspoon garlic powder
¼ teaspoon ground cinnamon
⅛ teaspoon ground nutmeg
1 pound ground raw turkey

● In a mixing bowl stir together egg, bread crumbs, olives, parsley, garlic powder, cinnamon, and nutmeg. Add ground turkey. Mix well.

Shape meat mixture into four ½-inch-thick patties. Place patties on the unheated rack of a broiler pan. Broil 3 to 4 inches from the heat for 5 minutes. Turn patties and broil for 4 to 6 minutes more or till no longer pink.

To eat or not to eat a burger? You won't have to ponder that question once you've caught a whiff of this classically Greek-flavored burger. It's true mealtime inspiration.

½ of a medium cucumber, very thinly sliced
4 hamburger buns, split
4 tomato slices
Plain yogurt *or* dairy sour cream
¼ cup crumbled feta cheese

● For *each* burger, place *one-fourth* of the cucumber slices on the bottom half of a bun. Top with a meat patty, tomato slice, some of the yogurt or sour cream, *one-fourth* of the feta cheese, and bun top. Serves 4.

Grilling directions: Prepare as above, *except* grill patties on an uncovered grill directly over *medium* coals for 5 minutes. Turn patties and grill for 4 to 5 minutes more or till done.

Catch of the day

Fish Fillets Olé

Fish Fillets Olé

Total Time: 20 minutes

4 *or* 8 frozen breaded fish
    fillets
¼ cup salsa
    Lettuce leaves
1 medium avocado, halved,
    seeded, peeled, and
    sliced

● Place fish fillets on the *ungreased* rack of a broiler pan. Broil 4 inches from the heat for 6 to 8 minutes or till heated through, turning after 3 minutes.

Meanwhile, in a small saucepan heat the salsa over medium-low heat till heated through.

To serve, place fish fillets on a lettuce-lined platter. Top with avocado slices and salsa. Makes 4 servings.

Before an avocado seed's slippery sliding act gets the best of you, try this trick to remove the seed. Use the cutting edge (not the tip) of a sharp knife to tap into the seed so the blade catches in it. Rotate the knife to loosen the seed and lift it out.

Herb-Buttered Fillets

Total Time: 20 minutes

1 pound fresh fish fillets *or*
    steaks
2 tablespoons margarine *or*
    butter
1 teaspoon finely shredded
    orange peel
1 tablespoon orange juice
¼ teaspoon fines herbes

● Cut fish fillets into 4 portions. Rinse fish and pat dry with paper towels.

For butter sauce, in a small saucepan melt margarine or butter. Stir in orange peel, orange juice, and fines herbes.

Think of fines herbes (pronounced FEEN zerb)— a savory blend of rosemary, sage, thyme, oregano, basil, and marjoram—as the convenience product with finesse.

  Salt
  Pepper
  Orange wedges

● Place fish fillets in a single layer on the greased unheated rack of a broiler pan or in a greased baking pan. Tuck under any thin edges. Brush fish with *half* of the butter sauce. Sprinkle the fish with salt and pepper.

Broil fish 4 to 5 inches from the heat till fish flakes easily when tested with a fork (allow 5 to 6 minutes for each ½ inch of thickness). If fish is more than 1 inch thick, turn when half done. Brush fish with remaining butter sauce during cooking. Garnish with orange wedges. Makes 4 servings.

Chili-Stuffed Peppers

Total Time: 15 minutes

1   15½-ounce can chili with
       beans
½   cup quick-cooking rice
¼   cup red salsa
2   teaspoons
       Worcestershire sauce

● In a 1½-quart microwave-safe casserole combine chili, rice, salsa, and Worcestershire sauce. Micro-cook, covered, on 100% power (high) for 3 to 5 minutes or till bubbly. Stir chili mixture. Cover and set aside.

2   medium green peppers
2   tablespoons water

● Meanwhile, cut green peppers in half lengthwise and remove seeds. Place pepper halves, cut side down, in an 8x8x2-inch microwave-safe baking dish. Add water. Cover with vented clear plastic wrap. Cook on high for 3 to 5 minutes or till the peppers are crisp-tender, giving dish a half-turn once. Drain the peppers, cut side down, on paper towels.

½   cup shredded Monterey
       Jack cheese with
       jalapeño peppers,
       (2 ounces)

● Arrange the pepper halves, cut side up, in the 8x8x2-inch baking dish. Spoon the chili mixture into the pepper halves. Cover with waxed paper.
    Cook on high for 2 to 3 minutes or till chili mixture is heated through, giving the dish a half-turn once. Sprinkle with cheese. Cook, uncovered, on high about 30 seconds or till cheese is melted. Makes 2 servings.

If you like fiery foods, use hot-style chili. If you prefer less spicy foods, use regular chili and substitute plain Monterey Jack cheese for the pepper version.

Attention, Microwave Owners

Recipes with microwave directions were tested in countertop microwave ovens that provide 600 to 700 watts of cooking power. Cooking times are approximate since microwave ovens vary by manufacturer.

Saucy Swiss Veal

Total Time: 15 minutes

1 tablespoon cooking oil
4 veal cubed steaks

● Preheat a 10-inch microwave browning dish on 100% power (high) for 5 minutes. Add cooking oil. Swirl to coat dish. Season veal with salt and pepper. Add veal to browning dish.

Micro-cook, uncovered, on high for 3 to 4 minutes or till no pink remains, turning veal over after 2 minutes. Transfer to serving platter. Keep warm.

½ cup milk
2 teaspoons all-purpose flour
1 2½-ounce can sliced mushrooms, drained
½ cup shredded process Swiss cheese (2 ounces)
1 tablespoon dried snipped chives

● For sauce, in a 2-cup microwave-safe measure combine milk and flour. Stir in mushrooms. Cook, uncovered, on high for 1 minute. Stir sauce. Cook for 1 to 2 minutes more or till sauce is thickened and bubbly, stirring every 30 seconds.

Stir in Swiss cheese and chives. Cook 30 to 60 seconds more or till cheese is melted. Spoon cheese sauce over veal steaks. Makes 4 servings.

To ensure a smooth cheese sauce every time, use process cheese.

Ham with Cucumber Sauce

Total Time: 10 minutes

1 1½- to 2-pound fully cooked ham slice

● Place ham in a 10x6x2-inch microwave-safe baking dish. Cover with waxed paper. Micro-cook on 100% power (high) for 8 to 10 minutes or till heated through, turning ham over after 5 minutes.

½ of a medium cucumber
1 8-ounce carton plain yogurt *or* dairy sour cream
1 tablespoon milk
1 teaspoon dried snipped chives
¼ teaspoon dried dillweed

● Meanwhile, chop the cucumber. In a small mixing bowl stir together cucumber, yogurt or sour cream, milk, chives, and dillweed. Serve cucumber mixture over ham. Makes 6 servings.

How do you cook a main dish in just 10 minutes and keep your cool, too? Try this ham slice with a refreshing cucumber and dill sauce.

Pork Chops Mirepoix

Pork Chops Mirepoix

Total Time: 25 minutes

2 **pork loin chops, cut ¾ inch thick**	● Trim excess fat from chops. Season with salt and pepper. In an 8x8x2-inch microwave-safe baking dish arrange chops with meatiest portions facing the outside of the dish. Cover with vented clear plastic wrap. Micro-cook on 30% power (medium-low) for 9 minutes.
	● Give the dish a half-turn and turn chops over. Cover with vented plastic wrap. Cook on medium-low for 10 to 12 minutes more or till meat is no longer pink. Keep warm.
1 **tablespoon margarine *or* butter** 1 **small onion, finely chopped (⅓ cup)** 1 **small carrot, finely chopped (⅓ cup)** ¼ **cup sliced fresh mushrooms** ¼ **teaspoon dried thyme, crushed** ⅛ **teaspoon ground red pepper** 2 **teaspoons dried parsley flakes**	● In a 1-quart microwave-safe casserole place margarine or butter. Cook, uncovered, on 100% power (high) for 35 to 40 seconds or till melted. Add onion, carrot, mushrooms, thyme, and red pepper. Cover and cook on high for 3 to 5 minutes or till vegetables are tender, stirring once. Stir in parsley. Spoon vegetable mixture over pork chops. Makes 2 servings.

Red pepper gives a little kick to this French-style dish. Mirepoix (mir PWA) refers to the sautéed vegetables and herbs.

Yogurt-Topped Lamb Chops

Total Time: 15 minutes

4 **lamb leg sirloin chops, cut ¾ inch thick**	● Trim excess fat from lamb chops. Season with salt and pepper. In an 8x8x2-inch microwave-safe baking dish arrange chops with the meatiest portions facing the outside of the dish. Cover with waxed paper. Micro-cook on 100% power (high) for 3 minutes. Turn chops over. Cook, covered, on high for 2 to 4 minutes more or till desired doneness.
¼ **cup plain yogurt** 1 **tablespoon brown sugar** ⅛ **teaspoon ground cinnamon** **Dash onion powder** **Snipped parsley (optional)**	● Meanwhile, for sauce, in a small mixing bowl combine yogurt, brown sugar, cinnamon, and onion powder. Spoon sauce over chops. Sprinkle with parsley, if desired. Makes 4 servings.

An easy, no-cook, cinnamon-charged sauce tops these micro-cooked lamb chops.

Cajun-Style Meat Ring

Total Time: 25 minutes

1 beaten egg
¾ cup soft bread crumbs
   (1 slice)
¼ cup milk
¼ cup finely chopped onion
½ teaspoon garlic salt
½ teaspoon dried thyme,
   crushed
   Several dashes bottled hot
   pepper sauce
1 pound ground beef

● In a large mixing bowl combine the beaten egg, bread crumbs, milk, onion, garlic salt, thyme, and hot pepper sauce. Add ground beef. Mix well.

To give our meat loaf a Louisiana flavor, we top it with a peppery tomato sauce and serve it with rice.

● In a 9-inch microwave-safe pie plate shape the meat mixture into a 6-inch ring that's 2 inches wide (see photo, below). Cover with waxed paper. Micro-cook on 100% power (high) for 7 to 9 minutes or till no pink remains and meat is done (170°), giving the dish a quarter-turn every 3 minutes. Transfer meat ring to a platter. Cover and keep warm.

1 8-ounce can tomato sauce
¼ cup chopped green pepper
¼ teaspoon celery seed
   Several dashes bottled hot
   pepper sauce
   Hot cooked rice

● For sauce, in a 2-cup microwave-safe measure combine tomato sauce, green pepper, celery seed, and hot pepper sauce. Cover with waxed paper and cook on high for 3 to 4 minutes or till green pepper is tender, stirring once. Spoon some sauce over meat. Serve with rice. Pass remaining sauce. Makes 4 servings.

To shape the meat ring, form the meat mixture into a mound 6 inches in diameter in the pie plate. Push the meat from the center to form a hole about 2 inches in diameter, making a 2-inch-wide meat ring.

Shortcut Gumbo

Total Time: 25 minutes

½ of a 10-ounce package
    frozen cut okra
1 14½-ounce can stewed
    tomatoes, cut up
1 6-ounce can spicy
    vegetable juice cocktail
1 tablespoon minced dried
    onion
2 teaspoons Worcestershire
    sauce
1½ teaspoons lemon juice
1 teaspoon instant chicken
    bouillon granules
½ teaspoon dried thyme,
    crushed
¼ teaspoon minced dried
    garlic
¼ teaspoon ground red
    pepper
¼ teaspoon ground allspice
1 bay leaf

● Thaw okra. In a 2-quart microwave-safe casserole combine okra, *undrained* tomatoes, vegetable juice cocktail, onion, Worcestershire sauce, lemon juice, bouillon granules, thyme, garlic, red pepper, and allspice. Add bay leaf.

    Micro-cook, covered, on 100% power (high) 6 minutes, stirring once.

Filé (pronounced fuh LAY) powder—powdered sassafras leaves—is a hallmark of many gumbos and other Creole dishes. Creole cooks add this seasoning after removing a dish from the heat so the filé won't string.

½ of a 16-ounce package
    frozen and deveined
    shrimp
3 ounces fully cooked ham,
    cut into ½-inch cubes
    (⅔ cup)
2 teaspoons filé powder
    Hot cooked rice

● Stir in shrimp and ham. Cook, covered, on high for 6 to 7 minutes or till shrimp turns pink, stirring twice. Remove bay leaf. Stir in filé powder. Spoon rice into soup plates. Ladle gumbo over rice. Makes 4 servings.

Easy Fajitas

Total Time: 25 minutes

1	**6-ounce container frozen avocado dip (optional)**

● If using frozen avocado dip, thaw it overnight in the refrigerator.

To speed this recipe, soften the tortillas in the microwave. Wrap them in plastic wrap. Micro-cook on 100% power (high) for 35 to 40 seconds or till they're soft.

8	**8-inch flour tortillas**
1	**pound ground beef**
1	**medium green pepper, cut into thin strips**
1	**small onion, thinly sliced**
½	**of a 0.7-ounce package dry Italian salad dressing mix**

● Wrap flour tortillas in foil. Warm in a 350° oven for 10 minutes.

Meanwhile, in a large skillet cook ground beef, green pepper, and onion about 5 minutes or till meat is brown and vegetables are tender. Remove from heat. Drain fat from skillet. Stir salad dressing mix into the meat mixture.

Red *or* green salsa
Dairy sour cream
Shredded cheddar cheese
Lettuce leaves *or* other greens

● Arrange the beef mixture down the centers of tortillas. Top with avocado dip, salsa, sour cream, and cheese. Roll tortillas around filling. Serve on lettuce-lined plates and top with additional dip, salsa, and cheese. Makes 4 servings.

Cheese-Beef Croissant
Sandwiches

Cheese-Beef Croissant Sandwiches

Total Time: 15 minutes

¼ cup mayonnaise *or* salad dressing 2 teaspoons horseradish mustard 1 teaspoon poppy seed ¼ teaspoon onion powder	● For dressing, stir together mayonnaise or salad dressing, mustard, poppy seed, and onion powder. Set aside.
4 croissants	● Split the croissants in half lengthwise. Spread the bottom half of each croissant with dressing.
4 lettuce leaves 8 ounces thinly sliced cooked beef 2 slices cheddar, Swiss, *or* Monterey Jack cheese, cut in half (3 ounces) ½ cup alfalfa sprouts	● Top each croissant bottom with lettuce, beef, cheese, and alfalfa sprouts. Top with croissant top. Serve with remaining dressing. Makes 4 servings.

Use the poppy seed dressing on other meat sandwiches, too.

Ham and Apple Sandwiches

Total Time: 10 minutes

1 3-ounce package very thinly sliced ham ½ of an 8-ounce container (½ cup) soft-style cream cheese ½ cup shredded cheddar cheese 1 small apple, chopped ⅛ teaspoon ground cinnamon	● Coarsely chop the ham. In a small mixing bowl stir together ham, cream cheese, cheddar cheese, chopped apple, and cinnamon.
6 slices whole wheat bread, toasted	● Spread half of the bread slices with the ham mixture. Top with remaining bread slices. Makes 3 servings.

This sandwich makes it easier for you to get your apple a day. We packed one into the ham and cheese spread.

Oriental Pork Sandwiches

Total Time: 20 minutes

¾ **pound pork tenderloin, cut crosswise into 4 pieces**
1 **tablespoon cooking oil**

● Place each piece of pork between 2 sheets of clear plastic wrap. Lightly pound with the flat side of a meat mallet to ¼- to ⅛-inch thickness.

Heat a large skillet over medium-high heat. Add the oil. Cook the pork for 4 minutes. Turn pork and cook 2 to 4 minutes more or till no longer pink. Remove the pork from the skillet.

2 **tablespoons sliced green onion**
2 **teaspoons sesame seed**
2 **tablespoons water**
2 **tablespoons dry sherry**
2 **tablespoons teriyaki sauce**

● For sauce, add green onion and sesame seed to drippings in the skillet. Cook, stirring constantly, about 1 minute or till sesame seed is toasted. Stir in water, sherry, and teriyaki sauce. Cook till heated through. Remove from heat.

4 **kaiser rolls, split and toasted**
Lettuce leaves *or* **shredded cabbage**

● To assemble sandwiches, top each roll bottom with lettuce or cabbage and pork. Drizzle some of the sauce over pork. Top with roll tops. Makes 4 servings.

These sandwiches are American, but their flavor is Oriental. For even more Oriental flavor, use bok choy or Chinese cabbage in place of the lettuce or cabbage.

Hot Sandwiches To Go

When you're on the run, choose one of these enticing sandwiches. They're quick to make and quick to eat.

● *Ham and Veggie Roll:* Cut a thin slice off the top of a *round club roll*. Hollow out the bottom, leaving a ½-inch shell. Pile very thin slices of *cooked ham* inside the roll bottom. Fill the roll with a drained *marinated vegetable salad* from the deli. Top with *Havarti cheese slices*. Broil a minute or two to melt the cheese. Recap with the roll top.

● *Beef and Slaw Barbecue Bun:* Toss bite-size strips of *cooked beef* with *barbecue sauce* mixed with a little *prepared horseradish*. Heat in a saucepan. Pile meat mixture onto the bottom of a split *hoagie roll*. Top with *coleslaw* and roll top.

● *Meat-Loaf Burrito:* Brush a *tortilla* with water to soften. Top with a *lettuce leaf* and *dairy sour cream*. Stack on *cooked meat loaf* and *cheddar cheese slices*, *avocado wedges*, and *onion slices*. Add *sweet pepper pieces* and *salsa*. Roll up. Fasten with a wooden toothpick. Heat in a microwave oven on 100% power (high) for ½ to 1 minute.

Manhattan Clam Sandwich

Total Time: 30 minutes

1 8½-ounce can whole
    white potatoes, chopped
1 6½-ounce can minced
    clams, drained
1 stalk celery, chopped
½ cup diced fully cooked
    ham
1 small tomato, seeded and
    chopped
½ cup sour cream dip with
    toasted onion
1 tablespoon dried parsley
    flakes
8 slices pumpernickel bread
    or 4 pita bread rounds,
    halved crosswise
    Shredded lettuce

● In a medium mixing bowl stir together potatoes, clams, celery, ham, and tomato. Add dip and parsley. Toss till coated.

    If using pumpernickel bread, spoon some of the clam mixture on *four* bread slices. Top with shredded lettuce and remaining slices of bread. If using pita rounds, line each pita half with some lettuce. Spoon some of the clam mixture into each. Makes 4 servings.

First, there was creamy New England clam chowder. Then came the Manhattan version with tomatoes. Now, here's the clam chowder sandwich—a clam-and-ham, potato-and-tomato filling served on bread or in a pita.

Greek Salad Pitas

Total Time: 25 minutes

2 tablespoons olive *or*
    salad oil
2 tablespoons wine vinegar
½ teaspoon dried oregano,
    crushed
⅛ teaspoon salt
⅛ teaspoon garlic powder

● For dressing, in a large mixing bowl stir together oil, vinegar, oregano, salt, and garlic powder.

1 2½- *or* 3-ounce package
    very thinly sliced
    chicken *or* turkey, cut
    into bite-size strips
1 cup shredded cabbage
1 small cucumber, chopped
1 small tomato, chopped
¼ cup sliced pitted ripe
    olives

● Stir in chicken or turkey, cabbage, cucumber, tomato, and olives. Toss well to coat with dressing.

½ cup crumbled feta cheese
¼ cup walnuts, coarsely
    chopped
    Lettuce leaves
3 pita bread rounds, halved
    crosswise

● Add cheese and walnuts. Toss lightly. Spoon chicken mixture into lettuce-lined pita halves. Makes 3 servings.

Question: Name the delicious Greek ingredients in this zesty sandwich.

Answer: Olive oil, oregano, cucumber, garlic powder, olives, feta cheese, walnuts, and pita bread rounds.

Meatball Drop Soup

Total Time: 35 minutes

1	**16-** *or* **20-ounce package frozen vegetables for stew**
1	**cup water**

● In a 3-quart saucepan combine frozen vegetables and water. Bring mixture to boiling. Reduce heat. Cover and simmer for 10 minutes.

Shaping meatballs is a cinch in this hearty soup. Just spoon the herb-flavored meat mixture into the simmering broth.

1	**beaten egg**
¼	**cup fine dry bread crumbs**
¼	**cup milk**
½	**teaspoon salt**
¼	**teaspoon dried marjoram, crushed**
1	**pound lean ground beef**

● Meanwhile, in a medium mixing bowl combine egg, bread crumbs, milk, salt, and marjoram. Add ground beef. Mix well. Set aside.

1	**15-ounce can herb tomato sauce**
1	**12-ounce jar brown gravy**

● Stir tomato sauce and gravy into vegetable mixture. Bring to boiling. Reduce heat. Drop beef mixture by small spoonfuls into the simmering mixture. Cover and cook for 10 to 12 minutes or till the meatballs are no longer pink and the vegetables are tender, stirring occasionally. Makes 5 servings.

Beer and Bean Chili

Total Time: 35 minutes

1 pound ground beef *or* pork
1 large onion, chopped (1 cup)
1 medium carrot, shredded (½ cup)
½ cup chopped green pepper

● In a Dutch oven cook ground beef or pork, onion, carrot, and green pepper till the meat is brown. Drain off fat.

2 15-ounce cans great northern beans
1 16-ounce can tomatoes, cut up
1 12-ounce can beer
1 6-ounce can tomato paste
2 tablespoons chili powder
½ teaspoon garlic salt

● Stir in *undrained* beans, *undrained* tomatoes, beer, tomato paste, chili powder, and garlic salt. Bring to boiling. Reduce heat. Cover and simmer for 15 to 20 minutes or till flavors are blended, stirring occasionally. Serves 5 or 6.

If you have any chili left over, freeze the extra. Reheat the chili in a saucepan. Or, if you have a microwave oven, heat, covered, on 70 percent power (medium-high), allowing 5 to 6 minutes per cup of chili.

Quick Beef-Noodle Soup

Total Time: 20 minutes

¾ pound beef top round steak
1 tablespoon cooking oil

● Cut the round steak into thin bite-size strips. In a large saucepan heat the oil over medium-high heat. Add the beef. Cook and stir for 3 to 4 minutes or till the beef is brown. Remove beef and set aside. Drain off fat.

1 3-ounce package Oriental noodles with beef flavor
4 cups beef broth
1½ cups loose-pack frozen mixed vegetables
1 cup water
1 stalk celery, thinly sliced
2 tablespoons soy sauce

● Break up the noodles. In the same saucepan combine noodles, seasoning packet, beef broth, mixed vegetables, water, celery, and soy sauce. Bring to boiling. Reduce heat. Cover and simmer about 5 minutes or till vegetables and noodles are tender. Stir in beef. Heat through. Makes 4 servings.

After adding the steak to the soup, cook the soup just enough to warm up the steak. Don't overcook or the meat will be tough.

Bratwurst-Cheese Soup

Total Time: 25 minutes

¼ cup margarine *or* butter
2 carrots, shredded
1 stalk celery, thinly sliced

● In a large saucepan melt the margarine or butter. Add carrots and celery. Cook till tender.

¼ cup all-purpose flour
⅛ teaspoon pepper
4 cups milk
8 ounces smoked bratwurst, sliced

● Stir in flour and pepper till blended. Add milk and bratwurst. Cook and stir over medium heat about 8 minutes or till mixture is thickened and bubbly. Cook and stir for 1 minute more.

2 cups shredded American *or* process Swiss cheese (8 ounces)

● Add cheese. Cook, stirring constantly, till cheese is melted. Makes 4 servings.

Chili-Beef Salad

Chili-Beef Salad

Total Time: 20 minutes

1 pound ground beef *or* bulk pork sausage
1 medium onion, chopped (½ cup)
1 7½-ounce can tomatoes, cut up
¼ cup catsup
1 tablespoon chili powder

● In a large skillet cook beef or sausage and onion till meat is brown. Drain fat from skillet. Stir in *undrained* tomatoes, catsup, and chili powder. Bring to boiling. Reduce heat and simmer, uncovered, for 8 to 10 minutes or till desired consistency.

Cool the spicy flavor of this taco-style salad with lots of sour cream. If you like a thinner dressing, stir a little milk into the sour cream.

4 cups shredded lettuce
1 cup shredded cheddar cheese (4 ounces)
8 pitted ripe olives, sliced
½ of an 8-ounce carton dairy sour cream
Snipped cilantro *or* parsley
Tortilla chips (optional)

● Arrange lettuce on each of 4 plates. Spoon meat mixture over lettuce. Sprinkle each with cheese and olives. Top with sour cream and cilantro or parsley. Serve with tortilla chips, if desired. Makes 4 servings.

Ham and Salami Slaw

Total Time: 30 minutes

½ of a 16-ounce package (4 cups) coleslaw mix
1 small zucchini, sliced
1 small onion, chopped

● In a large serving bowl combine coleslaw mix, zucchini, and onion.

Check out the produce aisle for a mixture of shredded cabbage and other vegetables packaged as a coleslaw mix. Or, make your own. Combine 3 cups shredded cabbage and 1 cup shredded carrot or other vegetables.

4 ounces thinly sliced fully cooked ham
4 ounces thinly sliced salami
1 4-ounce package (1 cup) shredded mozzarella *or* cheddar cheese

● Cut ham and salami into thin bite-size strips. Add ham, salami, and cheese to cabbage mixture. Toss lightly to mix.

½ cup creamy Italian salad dressing

● Pour dressing over salad. Toss lightly to coat. Makes 4 servings.

Chicken-Garbanzo Toss

Total Time: 35 minutes

1 15-ounce can garbanzo
   beans, drained
1½ cups cubed cooked
   chicken
2 stalks celery, sliced
1 small green pepper,
   seeded and chopped
2 green onions, sliced
   (optional)

½ cup mayonnaise *or* salad
   dressing
2 tablespoons lemon juice
¼ teaspoon chili powder
⅛ teaspoon onion powder
6 ounces shredded
   Monterey Jack cheese
   with jalapeño peppers
   (1½ cups)
   Lettuce leaves
1 tomato, cut into wedges
1 avocado, seeded, peeled,
   and sliced (optional)

● In a medium mixing bowl combine garbanzo beans, chicken, celery, green pepper, and, if desired, green onions.

● For dressing, in a small bowl combine mayonnaise, lemon juice, chili powder, onion powder, ¼ teaspoon *salt*, and ⅛ teaspoon *pepper*. Stir dressing into bean mixture. Stir in *half* of the shredded cheese. Chill in freezer about 15 minutes. Serve on lettuce leaves garnished with the remaining cheese, tomato wedges, and, if desired, avocado slices. Serves 4.

Just when you think there can't possibly be a new chicken salad, along comes our upscale green-pepper-and-garbanzo version. It's sure nice to be surprised every once in a while.

Cool Cuke Turkey Salad

Total Time: 25 minutes

½ cup dairy sour cream *or* plain yogurt
2 tablespoons mayonnaise or salad dressing
1 tablespoon milk (optional)
2 teaspoons dried dillweed *or* 2 tablespoons snipped fresh dillweed
1 green onion, sliced
¼ teaspoon pepper

● For dressing, in a small mixing bowl stir together sour cream or yogurt; mayonnaise or salad dressing; milk, if desired; dillweed; green onion; and pepper. Set aside.

Surprise guests? No worries. In just 20 minutes you can be sitting down to eat this tempting salad.

8 ounces smoked turkey breast portion, cut into ½-inch cubes
1 small cucumber, halved and thinly sliced
½ cup cashews *or* walnuts
Lettuce leaves *or* alfalfa sprouts

● In a medium mixing bowl combine turkey, cucumber, and cashews or walnuts. Pour dressing over all and toss to coat. Serve on lettuce leaves or alfalfa sprouts. Makes 3 servings.

Pita Pizza Salads

Total Time: 30 minutes

1 10-ounce package frozen chopped spinach
2 large pita bread rounds

● Cook spinach according to package directions. Drain, squeezing out excess liquid. Separate pita rounds into circles by slitting pitas around the outside and gently pulling apart the halves.

Pick this peck of pita pizzas, 'cause if you pick *these* pita pizzas, you'll have picked a pizza and a pretty salad, too!

½ of an 8-ounce container soft-style cream cheese with chives and onion
1 medium tomato, seeded and chopped (¾ cup)
¼ cup sliced pitted ripe olives
8 slices turkey ham, chopped

● Preheat the broiler. In a medium mixing bowl combine spinach, cream cheese, tomato, and olives. Toss to coat mixture well.
   Lay *one-fourth* of the chopped turkey atop *each* pita circle. Broil 3 inches from the heat for 1 minute. Spread *each* pita circle with *one-fourth* of the spinach mixture. Return to broiler for 1 minute.

1 cup shredded Swiss cheese (4 ounces)

● Sprinkle *one-fourth* of the cheese atop *each* pita circle. Broil about 2 minutes or till cheese starts to melt. Serves 4.

Index

Have BETTER HOMES AND GARDENS®
magazines delivered to your door.
For information, write to:
MR. ROBERT AUSTIN
P.O. BOX 4536
DES MOINES, IA 50336